Tread Softly

¤

Diana Woodcock

FUTURECYCLE PRESS
www.futurecycle.org

Cover artwork, "Flamingos at Sunset" by Betty Wills (Wikimedia Commons, License CC-BY-SA 4.0); author photo by U.S. Forest Service (Jacob Hofman photographer); cover and interior book design by Diane Kistner; Georgia text and titling

Library of Congress Control Number: 2017959048

Published by FutureCycle Press
Athens, Georgia, USA

ISBN 978-1-942371-48-9

Tread softly! All the earth is holy ground.

—Christina Georgina Rossetti

And forget not that the earth delights to feel your bare feet,
and the winds long to play with your hair.

—Kahlil Gibran

The worshippers of the Most Gracious are those
who tread the earth gently...

—Quran 25:63

Contents

PART FOUR
The Whole Wide Earth

PART ONE

The Arabian Desert

Learning to Tread Softly

To learn how to tread softly,
take counsel of the Bridled tern
on the open sea, resting
on any floating piece of debris
that's drifted its way.

Taking your heaviness away,
it'll make you light as one of its white
underwing feathers as it urges you
to merge with the salty air till you could
swear your body has disappeared.

Or observe the Swift tern
on an offshore island
laying its single egg
right onto the holy sand—
no need of a nest.

The lighter we tread,
the more we absorb
of earth's holiness—
each patiently soft footfall
giving birth to the fragile earth.

Explorations of evolutions,
geological holiness, fullness
and transience of Earth's wonders.
Holy ground trembling under
the weight of human mistakes—

whole landscapes laid to waste
by those who never learned to tread softly.
The secret is to feel the cord
binding you to the earth—to terns gracing
islands and coasts of the Red Sea,

Arabian Gulf. Never trudging,
always treading softly—believing
all of it is holy—even, especially,
when ravished by locusts, malaria-
carrying mosquitos, chlorpyrifos clouds.
Feet touching nothing as you levitate.
But wait—that isn't the goal,

to rise above it all. No, no, no.
You're missing the point.
Come back down to earth.

For what it's worth,
divinity can wait. Tread softly
among side-winding snakes and
desert rodents—gerbils, jirds, jerboas
who have nowhere else to go.

Feel every tendril and vein tingle
with intoxication of softly treading
over Aeolian sands—hummock
and barchan dunes, rocky hamadas,
wadis and runnels,

dune fields of coalesced barchans,
marine coastal sands of quartz.
All of it holy, holy, holy.
Tread softly, let the body—
merging with salt and air—disappear.

Lunchtime Along the Tideline

Cormorant flying
through shallows,
Little tern nose-dive bombing,

two whimbrels browsing
along the mudflats,
Grey heron gracing the edge,

flash of a sunlit silver fish.
Noon-bright high tide,
stars and Pink Moon hide.

Inland, a sand dune shifts.
Far out at sea, a Hawksbill
turtle lifts his eyes to the skies—

glides in silence past seaweed,
eels, feathery polyps, butterfly fish—
its buried eggs long forgotten.

And where are you in all this?
Dreaming drifter drawing circles
at the edge, shifting

into the intuitive mode,
waiting for the moon's coolness.
Floating, rising, gliding

as if set free from gravity's
and time's constraints.
Moving with ease and fluidity

you've only known in dreams.
Till now. But the instant
you realize and would hold on

for dear life, your heavy feet
pull you back down to earth,
up to the surface

though you long to go right on
drifting and shifting
with all the luminous ones.

Nearly Paradise

Nearly paradise:
the oil-rich Gulf.
But diesel run-off's
turning gift into devastation.

The desert fox skirting
toxic sludge like a pro,
alerting you to truth.
Go out and shadow it,

inhale the poisonous smell,
admit this is as close to hell
as one might get
this side of paradise.

Of course this could be
nothing more than speculation,
opinion. What is absolute?
Yellow-tinged horizon no less truth

than the Crested lark's singing
over wadis and jebels,
and the curative powers
of each desert herb.

The shamal whirling smoke
from oil flares everywhere
while you devotedly seek out
wildflowers after the first
winter rains. Rampant

the desert's proliferation
to the point of intoxication
for the one who lingers long
at attention while the greening

persists, oblivious to the fact
(truth) of toxic fumes and other
dangers of the produce of crude
oil and liquefied natural gas.

Nature persisting in time of
environmental abuse.
Absolute truth. God bless
this man-infested desert.

Protect it for the spiny-tailed
lizard and blue-headed agama,
for the camels and oryxes,
Persian nightingales and Pallid swifts,

wildflowers and herbs, this
one Desert White now sipping
sustenance from *Pulicaria*—
another instance (insistence) of truth.

The Dicots

Everything that seems empty is full of the angels of God.
—St. Hilary

Best time and place to perceive
the radiance of mind's true nature:
hour preceding dawn in the desert

before day prevails over night,
bringing everything to light.
All seeming at first deserted.

But look closer: the annual herb
devil's thorn thriving, its flowers
ripening under the surface;

the delicate thread-stem carpetweed
donning its green flowers.
In every depression along margins

of cultivated land, in shady moist places,
on dry salines, Her most advanced floral plants
stretching your boundaries to the max.

Fullness of the presumably empty desert
surrounding you, holy presences abounding there,
you'll never want to leave, having reached

deep inside where the center holds.
Hour before dawn, words having lost all
meaning, you'll float across the Empty Quarter

like a Mute swan, oblivious to time,
trailing your toes through drifted sand,
heaven under your feet, each formation—

shamal-sculpted—rising
like a jubilant proclamation.
You'll hear an angel applauding

each flower ripening
as your mind's true radiance shines
bright as the Harvest Moon.

Desert Monitor Lizard

(Varanus griseus)

In one moment spent observing
the endangered fork-tongued

Desert Monitor as it suns
itself on a kopje, the emptiness

of worldly existence overwhelms.
Silence, stillness astounds.

Time to trade in my downy bed
for a hard lodging.

Tired of living half-dead,
keep my eyes wide open—

find my own flat-topped
solitary spot in the sun.

Jazirat Umm Tais Preserve

*barrier island northern tip of Qatar,
east from Ruwais*

My feet still tingling from wading
through a tidal channel, rich mud
of the mangroves, they now move
to the rhythm of Fleetwood Mac:
Rhiannon, Landslide, Over My Head.

Spent the day among cyanobacteria
and blooming *Suaeda vermiculata.*
I turned around, and the water
was closing all around like a glove...
How could I ever withdraw my love
from this world's bounty?

I walked across poisonous mats,
breathed in their toxins. No
apparent harm, no need for alarm.
So many locals suffering from asthma
and other congestive conditions.

I thought of Kimiko Hahn's calf poem
about polluted Patancheru,
India—toxins leaking from broken
pipelines, industrial waste dumped
in public places. But here, the people have
wealth—money buying them everything
except good health, clean air to breathe.

Earth's woes all around them,
desert too much with them,
the shamal laying toxins at their feet,
in their lungs, their hearts given away
to *getting and spending.*
The world is too much with us.

I strolled over microbial mats,
over blue-green algae, unicellular
cyanobacteria—photosynthetic
organisms unique to Qatar,
abundant due to extreme heat,
strong sunlight, highly saline waters.

Primitive life form found in intertidal sediment,
surface crusts along beaches,
coastal mangroves, brown sabkhas—
binding desert sands,
providing carbon and nitrogen,
supporting plant communities,
reducing wind and water erosion.

I tread softly on intertidal algal mats
near Jazirat, following trails of
mangrove whelk—mud creepers and
crabs, brackish water snails—
winding through mangroves
with aerial roots in the salt marsh.

Mangrove Forest, Umm Tais National Park

A stand of dead coral extends
from Qatar's northern tip,
where two barrier islands are forming—

halophytes proliferating,
Grey mangrove dominating,
the other salt-tolerant ones

just as reverent: Desert hyacinth,
Bean caper, Sea lavender,
saltwort and sedge.

To get up close and personal,
wade across a tidal channel.
You'll hear them, the mangroves,

breathing through their long horizontal
roots that shoot up spikes
through saline mud—pneumatophores.

In this coastal salt marsh habitat,
an erect-ascending shrub offering
capsules to be pounded up in milk—

an aphrodisiac for Bedouins.
Ah, the botany of desire: sweet
breathing of mangroves. No,

you must not gaze at them from the shore.
You must get your feet wet—let
them sink into tiny holes of ghost crabs.

Tread softly, tip-toe—minnows among
aerial roots. And mud creepers—
whelks, snails, mollusks.

Birds and bees among the leaves
and tiny flowers, grey to match the mud.
Halophytes—those heroes of *halos*

thriving where most cannot,
excreting salt through tiny holes
in leathery leaves, or simply shedding

salt-stuffed foliage. Bowing down
in a most profound show of reverence.
If we heed their example,

we could be transformed—
sinner to saint, the quaint life
of mangroves and their brethren halophytes.

Immeasurable, what they give us—
their serenity to be envied.
How irreverent my painted toenails

against the grey of saline mud.
A blessing—how else to consider them?—
gracing this intertidal zone.

Like coming home, feeling welcomed
here among them. Do you not see it,
feel it—the shimmering radiance—

this tidal channel filling you with a delight
you thought you'd never feel again?
What more evidence could you need?

Prayer Before Going Out into the Desert to Find Wildflowers

Dear Gaia, your desert adorned now
with delicate blossoms—seed colonies
called forth by winter rains,

may I tread softly, silently
so as to disturb neither sand fish
nor blue-headed agama.

Guide me to rock crevices,
dunes, fossil corals, granite
outcrops, sandy wadis, drifted

sands of this desolate harsh land.
May I go with a haiku mind,
determined to take my time—

noticing the way subtle petals display
their beauty midday for the bees alone.
Among wildflowers, beyond

mid-winter's thunder, far from
terrorism, let me marvel how the fragile
flowers stand up to the oil flare and noon sun.

Dear Gaia, refresh them before I come;
let the dawn mists baptize each leaf
and stem, entice each bud to spread wide

its exuberance to the new day.
Lead me to where sea lavender
graces the shore. Give me eyes to see

the Cape hare hunkered down
in the midst of a salt bush
or wind-blown sandy hummock.

Let me take nothing for granted—
not even abundant inconsequential
salt bushes with their faint yellow tinge.

Among red *arta*, I'll keep
a compassionate eye out
for the sleeping scorpion.

If I could see *Capparis spinosa* or
Silene villosa, that desert campion,
I would be most grateful.

And *Citrullus colocynthis*—
desert squash prostrating itself
across hard sand. And one little set

of footsteps imprinted by the patterings
of a Baluchistan gerbil or Libyan jird,
it'd be more than worth the trip.

Though I become wind burnished,
let me stay till the winter sun sets
and nocturnal ones—unafraid

of a little frost—venture forth.
You have my word: I shall honor
every life form I encounter.

I shall kneel silently
beside each flower, reverently
in awe, emptying a little of myself

into each perfect floret
till there is none of me
to bring back.

Every August,

the desert Hades-hot,
brown leaves whirling
in my grim garden—

all dust and decay,
no chance of rain till winter—
I wonder why I stay.

But I embrace it, cozy up to it
like a welcome fire on a wintry day—
Cape hare in a clump of singed saltbush.

No, I don't wish for a way out.
I sit facing the hot *suhaili* wind,
in the sidra's shade, listening

to a Persian nightingale's song—
under its spell every fear quelled.
I inhale the wafting scent of desert

hyacinth, drift into the realm
of serenity. But no, I must go
further: step into the unknown,

a gap—Bardo, Tibetans call it—where
nothing is certain save spaciousness
to swallow me up—my belly of the whale;

step into the gap between sky and sea,
like a silver Sea bream breaking free,
rising out of its watery world,

defying gravity. Forget
self, expand with hope
till in rapture I leave this world—

fragment like fireworks,
become all fire—
to find a thousand new ones.

Home in the Arabian Desert Biome

Even this hard-packed, cracked
ground in August, which it would take
a miracle for that deep blue prickly herb
Blepharis ciliaris to break through,
as it will in winter when the Rain

goddess waves her wand over Arabia.
My body a microcosm of this dot
of the universe—dry skin, cracked heels,
mind and spirit parched as well.
Heat of the desert, beat of my heart—

we move in unison toward autumn.
Wind propels oleander branches to fan
the feral cats panting in their shade.
I fan myself in empathic symbiosis,
breathing the same stifling air,

planted in the same parched yet
holy ground across which the Spiny-
tailed lizard stretches, in its element,
recharging its body as it soaks up
August sun. Earth holy home,

a Scarab beetle emerges from the smallest
black hole around, and I think yes,
how marvelous are the galaxies,
comets, hidden seas on Saturn's moon.
But just now, this biome's all I need—

cracked, hard-packed though it be,
its mercy in the shape of tunnels
into which dhubs, gerbils and jirds escape
to wait out August till little by little,
the temperatures drop, the mists begin

to dispense their revelation (salvation)
drop by drop onto the acacia,
desert scrub, the agama's blue head,
wings of the clamorous warblers
rising from their mangrove stands.

PART TWO

The Everglades

Everglades: Day One

Here for only one month,
I'll say it at the outset: I won't go
until I see the snakes King and Indigo.
Although the ultimate goal's not merely
to see but become a part of the Everglades—
spend my days just being in the very midst
of it, this the gist of it:

lazing away a part of each day dozing
under the pond apple tree with alligator,
pig frogs chanting their lullabies nearby;
drifting with Florida gar—unconcerned
with going far; staying alert—finding a way
to interpret sloughs and solution holes,
to engage with quiet surfaces—the subtleties
of June; creeping as slowly as the grassy
river flowing south; marveling at what each
component's all about.

No doubt the voice of hope rings louder
here than that of despair. I hear it everywhere:
sense of wonder reawakened, sense of awe as
eyes have taken in vast expanses of sawgrass.
Listening with ears and heart, I hear the Earth
speaking in whispers and gestures—or loudly
and clearly in roars of male alligators, snorts
of pig frogs, harsh calls of marshbirds, whistles
of wind through swaying sawgrass.

I have come, as Job suggested, to ask panther,
anhinga, gar fish and alligator to teach me.
I have loosened my hair as Li Po instructed
and now linger in a place where water flows
imperceptibly to the sea *though we cut it*
with our swords. I stand quietly like a stalking
bittern blending with sawgrass. I have come to
wake and sleep in the Everglades' arms, to sit
at its feet that it might set me on fire, after which
I'll go back and ignite minds and hearts with
one spark.

Pa-hay-okee

Grassy waters beguiled me
(too long caught up in black holes,
exploding stars, the mystical sphere)
back down to Earth: sawgrasses;
and between blades, an ever so
slowly rising, flowing river—

Earth's circulatory system draining
into the Gulf of Mexico,
Atlantic Ocean, evaporating back
into the atmosphere,
water composed of alligators' tears.
Sawgrasses swaying and setting tiny

blades against the rainy season's
wind. Courageous egrets tip-toeing
through shiny sharp edges of
golden-green sedges.
Swamp lilies trembling among
gar and anhingas. Lingered

among them, endangered
if need be as the ones struggling
to survive: Cape Sable Seaside
sparrow, West Indian manatee,
Wood stork,
Florida panther,

Indigo snake, American
crocodile, Apple snail
in this massive watershed—
America's largest sawgrass
prairie—where I came
back down to Earth.

Beggar in the Everglades

What is to give light must endure burning.
—Viktor Frankl

It pierces my heart till I rejoice when the mosquito pricks
my finger for blood to nurture her eggs, initiating me into
the life cycle of this place to which I've come like meeting
someone for the first time and feeling I've known her
all my life. They tell me their life story, and I'm converted—
born again—their waters, slow-moving shallow river rising
with summer rain, baptize me. And I'm forgiven—sins
of omission (failing to do the little I could do to protect
and restore them)—draining, bulldozing of their sawgrass
prairies. Washed in the blood of a million plume birds,
I offer my body to be bitten, slashed, burned, but they
neither punish nor scold; they are gentle, delicate even in
their pain, in their sentient struggle to regain their rightful place.
Sovereign in tenacity, endurance of extremes: drought, deluge,
plenty, starvation, disaster. Symbol of fortitude, rainbow
after the storm. Stasis in the mangroves, pivot of manatee
and speedboat. I walk softly, silently—afraid of killing,
injuring, disturbing anything in this fragile place.
Red-winged blackbird taking over my favorite post
and alligator dozing on my path remind me *I'm* the intruder—
here today, gone tomorrow. I lift up my bowl for them to fill,
walk humbly through sword-sharp sawgrass by the slough,
admiring the slender beauties heaven-made: egret, heron,
anhinga, ibis, wood stork, bittern, limpkin.
I pray for their flame that I might burn through
the dark night and give light. Let a green bird—heron
preferred—descend on my head if indeed I am the elect.
Let me make collyrium for my eyes from the dust kicked up
by the alligator, that I might see more clearly and die pure.
Let the roseate spoonbill transform my soul into pure gold.
Then, great egret—delicate as falling snow—send me forth
as arrow to pierce hearts set on destruction.

In the Company of Alligators

They were the last thing
I went to see—could not
imagine what the attraction
could be. I went for birds:
anhingas, spoonbills, egrets,
herons. And swamp lilies.
Manatees and dark, steamy
mangroves. Maritime fauna.
Palmetto palms and pig frogs.
Whispering of wind across
sawgrass prairies.

But from the moment I spotted
that first one dozing along
Anhinga Trail, I was hooked.
Hearing the bellowing of two
echoing across the slough—a
sutra—I knew they were saints
if not prophets, beyond good
and evil, soul-readers seeing by
God's light, wildly created,
audacious, hypnotic, driven
forward by practicalities—not
hostilities, in control—rulers but
not dictators of the slough, kings
of the vast river of grass, a dark
tense presence, unadulterated motion
among soft-shelled turtles, garfish
and fallen ripened pond apples.

Sinking deep into my awareness,
triumphantly fulfilling my need
for distinct, unabashed wildness.
Even here, back now in my desert,
the Everglades flows through my days,
bellows of alligators like plain chants
echo in my ears—rhapsody, love song
so endearing, drowning out the
groaners of this sad world.

Hosanna to the alligators
in the highest: Glory be
to their Maker.

Entering,

In the beginning was the Word...
—John 1:1

my soul was pierced—never
expecting the toll it would take.
Yet by the end transformed, reborn,
baptized in her sloughs and rains—
all sins committed against her

forgiven. Heaven waiting:
Snowy egret, Great white heron,
Glossy ibis angels gliding overhead
or standing patiently forever in the
wet Jamaica sawgrass.

And so I sloshed into the grassy river,
followed alligator tracks over marl and
peat popups, brushed edges sharp as razor
blades, allowed Swamp lilies to swab
my blood and tears, egrets and limpkins

directing me to *Step here,* Pig frogs
grunting on spatterdock leaves, hunting
for their very own piece of the sky.
Fire and rain, drought and drainage,
she renews herself again and again,

surviving man's latest scheme.
Ashes after controlled burns highlighting
her contours like collyrium encircling
Bedouin women's eyes.

Strolling among alligators and garish-
colored Lubber grasshoppers, fears
were allayed by the light that dispels
deepest darkness, moving through dots,
circles, spots—bewildering black in its

frigid opacity, Gnostic red, then tranquil
heavenly green—emerald Everglades
teaching the heavenly names of things,
angelic half of my soul revealed.

When the grasshopper crawled out
of the flames, crossed the road
to the side not slated for a prescribed
burn, heart yearned for the beginning
when the Word was.

Prairies glowing like ovens, like heavens.
Black powder, Everglades ash ingested
for brighter vision. Soot of burnt,
shelled almond encircling my eyes.
The light of the body is the eye.

Existence Is Light

> *What will the world be once bereft*
> *of wet and wildness? Let them be left.*
> —Gerard Manley Hopkins

Nowhere have I heard it more clearly,
Beginning's Word, past still being spoken
by alligator and whippoorwill. Nowhere
have I seen as radiant a light as that
reflecting off tawny sawgrass where
that master of illumination, great white heron,
stands in the niche for lights.

I've traveled to Aleppo and studied
theosophical Sufism, but only in the Everglades
did it finally make sense: existence is light—
light equally illuminating green and brown.

Slogging in my Wellingtons across prairie
through moat onto hardwood hammock where
the strangler fig launched a shimmering seed at me,
the five-lined skink shined metallic blue as light
called it forth out of its slumber,

I would remain silent and celibate
if I could end my days among Sufi master
snowy egret, angel roseate spoonbill,
the hunched Han poet green heron. I would
stay awake, I would meditate—let the light
illuminate life moving above and through
the river of grass.

I would not ask for rain in dry season—
only for light, and to enter into the wildness
and wet—to do nothing more or less than
reflect it as perfectly as the snowy egret's
three-egged nest braced on a cardinal airplant
proliferating on a dwarf cypress.

Kin to All of Nature

Surrounded by the grassy river, finally
becoming *plants, trunks, foliage, roots, bark,*
I caught Walt Whitman's meaning.

Became a coral, a sponge at home on the hard
marine bottom, a succulent on a coastal prairie
beyond the mudflats. Became the tallest conifer
of a cypress dome, quite at home in standing water.

Became the twirled strangler fig on a gumbo limbo,
the peeling bark the trunk curled back in protest,
the acid from a decaying plant dissolving limestone
around a hardwood hammock, helping make the moat.

Became the soil collecting in the jagged bedrock,
the root of a slash pine taking its time breaking through
the crack, the outer bark of the pine scorched by fire
sweeping across a limestone ridge. Became one blade
of golden green sawgrass swaying as if praying
for one songbird to perch and sing its praises to sky
and prairie. Became the haven of shade in the hum of
the hammock, the five-lined teal-tailed skink poised
on the rail, listening and waiting. Became the wide
grassy river, the wetness of summer, seagrass sheltering
shellfish. Became a coastal channel, mangrove forest,
the stilt-like roots of one red mangrove.

Became marl sediment settled on the limestone
of a freshwater prairie, allowing slow seepage of water.
Became the deeper faster-flowing center of that broad
marshy river, the panther prowling on hidden hammocks
through the night, the thunder cloud spilling out its
blessing summer afternoons. Became the alligator
sunning on Taylor Slough's bank, pond apple plopping
into the silently flowing, rising river, zebra swallowtail
dreaming on the string lily, fanning my wings.

Became water defying human borders—vapor
moving invisibly, liquid percolating through peaty
soil and marl.

Became myself again as I once was in the
beginning—present to and kin to all of nature.

Celestial Cathedral

Heaven is under our feet as well as over our heads.
—Henry David Thoreau

Every configuration
of cloud and mangrove,
each endangered Cape Sable
seaside sparrow, Florida

panther, manatee,
crocodile, hardwood
hammock, slough.
Disguised angels:

ibis, heron, egret shining
light on sawgrass prairies,
lending hallelujahs and
mandolas at dusk to frogs.

No barren soil—epiphytes
feeding on nothing but air and
sunlight, growing on mahogany
and Pond apple trees.

Alligators and Roseate spoonbills
revealing a place wounded by man,
forgiving as rain falls
from the upper chamber.

If You Doubt

If you doubt,
go out to where
Snowy egret stands
among Swamp lilies.
Wait silent and still

like it, and listen
as each frog
takes up its chant.
Watch how sun sinks
into sawgrass marsh,

and the afterglow
smoothes out the slough's
rough edges.
Watch Mother Alligator
guarding her young

though they have flung
themselves far and wide
just now. Listen
to Green heron scolding
them; watch how he leans

toward the dark waters,
spits out a bit of Pond apple—
luring a Killifish.
Notice when Snowy egret
spears a Grass frog,

silence reigns as Creation,
in unison, awaits the light
of a new day when nothing
will kill in Her holy slough.

Obligation (Sermon in the Margins)

> *Holiness is not a luxury reserved for the*
> *few, but an obligation for us all.*
> —Mother Teresa

They make it seem so easy, the ones
on stilted legs along lagoons and mangroves,
on mudflats and coral shoals—

being wholly what they are, devoted
to the work of their creator, displaying
a spirit of *share and share alike,* aware

it would seem of their dependence
on the earth, not obsessed with their own
worth. What better form of gratitude?

Observing these feathered saints,
I feel ashamed—hoarding and taking
more than my share. Aspire anew,

I urge myself, to cool all desire,
repent of crimes that set me apart
from them: greed and ambition,

quarrelsomeness and disobedience.
Yet would I trade consciousness
for their peace of wildness?

September Prayer for the Everglades

Three in one: Ramadan,
Rosh Hashanah nearing the
day of atonement, Feast
of our Lady of Sorrows—day
to mourn species extinction,
pray for the endangered ones:

snail kite, Cape Sable Seaside
sparrow, Florida panther.
Forget about the six ways
of reincarnation. Not bound
by sects and creeds, their home

the only preferred place of
worship—no need of synagogue
or mosque. Let me return and
stay, walk silently with a little
broom, or with my eyelashes,

sweeping the threshold of these
saints. Neither miner nor bat,
I'm claustrophobic among
dripping stalactites, but between

sawgrass and slough, I blossom
and ignite like a New Year's Eve
sparkler.

I've been to Tibet,
Thailand and Greece—
thought I'd died and found
heaven within reach,

until the River of Grass
whispered my name, which
no one had pronounced
correctly since childhood.

The Cell or Desert versus the Everglades

> *Go sit in your cell, and it will teach you everything.*
> —Abba Moses, Desert Father

I thought it was true,
I so wanted it to be—
tired of traipsing around the world
chasing after elusive things.
But the Everglades beckoned,
and I reckoned it wouldn't hurt—
needed a respite from the desert.

It was like treading the middle path
between the world's vacuity and reality.
Faint scent of skunk, smoldering
pines, lubber grasshopper crawling
out of the ashes, Liguus tree snails
keeping to their task along straight
and narrow smooth-barked trails.

Elusive panther's seen it all before,
keeping careful score—can't be
spooked, its bravado fail-proof.
Fragile yet enduring, its light
penetrating the darkest night.
Swamp lily and great white heron
rising from grass that can slash like a knife.

The cell may teach me well—may
even preach—but only when I lifted
my eyes, held out my hand to touch
the cardinal airplant cradled in the crook
of the mahogany did I rise up,
leaving myself behind, to touch the face
of God.

The cell may once again teach me,
sheltering me from desert's harshness,
and I will sit and attempt to take it
all in, though my heart has dropped a seed

into the head of the cabbage palm
and is sprouting there between strangler
fig and gumbo limbo, becoming pure
light and air, setting brush fires—flamed
by flamingos and ghosts of a million plume
birds—in contented people's hair.

PART THREE

Misty Fiords

Temperate Rainforest

Another rainy day, exotic
in its own way. Rhythm of drops
on cabin's skylights and roof,
waterfall at our doorstep flowing
faster than yesterday. A Swainson's
thrush singing its little heart out above
the rush of waterfall and rain.

On the tiny island in the lake a Glaucous-
winged or Mew gull sits on its nest just
as its ancestors have done here two million
years or more. The last glacial advance
requiring equilibrating—Yellow and Western
Red cedar moving north from California.
Wind, not fire, the more disturbing element—

multiple canopy of layers and ages. Indeed,
forests perpetuated by wind always tend
to be more complex. An abundance
of snags and logs, one half of its mass.
Yellow and Western Red cedars more than one
thousand years old; Sitka spruce, Western and
Mountain hemlock more than five hundred.

In this the world's most extensive,
impressive temperate rainforest, acknowledge
nature as audible. Be humbled, filled with
empathy and hope as you listen and observe.
Laying aside all mapping and naming,
measuring and shaping, simply be with
and of this most magnificent forest.

Alone in natural splendor, become
American dipper walking under the waterfall,
baptized again and again, making
of your small fragile life a light.

In the Spray Zone of Waterfalls,

thriving ferns—Western Maidenhair,
delicate deciduous fronds blading up
eighteen inches long and broad,
shiny deep-brown leaf stalks

fit for native baskets. Ecstatic,
you watch, feel altered, fully alive
for the first time in too long a while
as rushing water sways the spore-bearers,

your six senses fully attuned,
thrill of itinerancy—eco-
location and dispossession—
you would thrive as a Maidenhair fern,

rooted in the spray zone beside Manzanita
Lake, Misty Fiords—your other life
of desert dwelling a mirage.
You would smuggle your heart

into that still space—eye of waterfall—
American dipper occupies as it walks
underwater among the erect
vascular plants' petioles.

Dare not look away, now the day
of salvation, ferns that sway all
the world you need. Behold, you flourish
though the obscure sun absents itself

from this rainforest, the lace
of the ferns' fronds a delicate
lavish grace on each moist rock face.
Soft rain, cascading snowmelt—

wet glistening of lush ferns
beside which you envision and yearn
for the other side of the falling,
dissolving.

Winstanley Lake, Revillagigedo Island

Tlingits, Haidas, Tsimshians
first came here to trap mink and otter,
hunt seals. We paddle out mid-morning—
sun warming, melting snow on peaks.
Cutthroat trout and Sockeye salmon
swimming about, a lone loon preening,

Dwarf dogwood and Salmonberry
blooming along the shore,
Witch's Hair and Old Man's Beard
wisping from cedars, spruces, hemlocks.
Old stumps and logs blushing with
pale pink Fairy barf.

Surrounded by snow fields, glaciers,
mist, we inhale deeply—all around us
a softness like satin, save for ginseng's
cousin, that thorny Devil's club.
Sitka alders marking shore, avalanche tracks.
Tall Bluebells embellishing stream bank,

wet meadow. Saplings emerging from
nurse logs. Rocks smoothed by mosses
where seeds germinate. All these
terrestrialized entities working magic
on the heart, I feel at home—everything
familiar, convivial as I'm taken in by a land

so lush and luminous I feel it again,
that sense of insignificance, how it all
will go on without me. Left alone
with cliff face and lake, I could bear
the world's weight, needing only one
Devil's club stick for a charm.

Nooya Lake

Following tracks and scat
of a Brown (Grizzly) bear,
we made our way from float plane
to shore over muddy trail to shelter,
surrounded by Skunk cabbage

and flowers of Salmon and Blueberry
(on which one Rufus hummingbird dined).
A Varied thrush sang to us each night,
rang a wake-up call each dawn.
Day one we canoed the lake

from which granite walls of stone—
rounded sheer cliffs—rose up,
snow-draped this late June (a dolly
of lace to grace the peak), the loon pair
calling, answering their own echo

again and again as we drifted late
afternoon. We, like the loons,
the only pair of our kind on the whole lake.
Sound of waterfalls, Glaucous gulls
crying when we paddled too close to their nest.

Day two, we hiked into summer
through an old-growth forest—where
Methuselah's Beard hung from Hemlocks,
Yellow and Red cedars—to the ocean
where it lived up to its name (Pacific),

where we sat on mossy ground in a meadow
of Black lilies, buttercups, Indian paintbrush—
around which snow-crowned rounded peaks
glistened as we listened to the tide rising.
Summer Solstice, what better way to spend the day

than in the heart of a temperate rainforest.
After days of rain, the sun all day.
I paid rapt, animal attention
that I might be put back "in complicity
with things as they happen."

With only one intent, I went
into the forest, onto the lake—
to interact with wildlife,
intuit and imagine, be at bear's
and loon's disposal, communicate

with the vegetable world that I might be
transformed—my autonomous self
joined in holy matrimony
with ecological matter.
Having basked in *Systema Naturae*

in all its glory—beasts, birds,
plants—I came away convinced
Homo sapiens will no time soon
hold a candle to Brown bear,
Devil's club, or loon.

Wild Wet Harmony

Oh let them be left, wildness and wet;
Long live the weeds and the wilderness yet.
—Gerard Manley Hopkins

Each square foot a station
of the cross. Listen
and observe the flowing,
falling of waters—rain,
melting snow, primordial sound
to drown out the next round
of suicide bombings.
Along the unswept muddy path,
you do the math:
violence plus more violence,
an eye for an eye equals a world
gone mad and blind. But here,
where all lives in wild, wet harmony—
taking only enough to survive—
you could thrive, eyes and ears open wide
to the wonders: Toy soldiers
(*Cladonia bellidiflora*) on rotting
stumps and logs; Fragrant Wood
ferns on rocky bluffs, talus and scree
slopes; Devil's club, that perennial
yellow-spiny shrub. Nature
providing all the grandeur
a world at war lacks.
No distance separating self
from all the others. Primed by
cascades of waterfalls and loons' calls,
the body inclines toward wildness
and wet—only one regret:
the salmon have not yet
begun their run. Bears not yet
lined up along the falls waiting
patiently, feasting persistently
in the midst of wet wildness—
a pulsing, indivisible bridge
from which one could throw over

the ego and dwell forever
in the Beautiful Beyond,
each square foot a station
to lighten the load,
refresh spirit, replenish
heart and soul. Reaching
the source of wildness and wet,
drink till thirst is quenched.
Breathe in the air of creation—
all things new where the dead
and dying nurture new life.
No need to unfurl prayer rugs here—
moss-softened ground as holy as it gets.
No need to pray five times a day.
The one becomes unending, without
ceasing for Damascus, Aleppo, Gaza
and all the other burning cities.
Oh let them be left—the Salmon and
Blueberry bushes, the thrushes
who sing their praises to the wet
wildness dawn and dusk.

Conducting Research in Misty

The dangers of life are infinite,
And safety is among them.—Goethe

You have escaped one of life's
infinite dangers—safety—to come
face to face with a White Rein orchid.
Now you rest among them,
having flung aside all fear.
Here you've found all you need
to know. *Beauty is truth,*

truth beauty, the Black lily.
Nothing enters your thoughts
but joy. Stream violet edging forest.
Strands of Witch's hair gracing old
growth trees, conifers and hardwoods.
A cool breeze across the meadow.
Five-leafed bramble scrambles
over the ground. *Truth is one.*

Devil's club. Stink currant.
Gravity holding you to the dazzling place
where Rosy Twisted Stalks rise up resilient,
restoring your resolve to pay attention,
let nature's muscle power your own.
Escaping into the wild wetness,
the green chaos of Misty—Bunch-
berry, Deer fern—you learn the terrain,
let it sustain. Siberian Miners lettuce.

This is no mere scenic background,
Misty no helpless victim.
You interact with one spruce,
three hundred and thirty-four years old
when it fell, Fall 2010. It began
1680 A.D., Nooya Creek drainage,
in a clearing left by an ancestor,
a century's old spruce downed
in a windstorm. Sensing your ancestry,
read (like a prayer book) the leaves
and petals of the Western Starflower.

This teeming rainforest, steaming mists—
what if your soul could transmigrate
right here and now, in a flash, past
Purple violets' intimation of cremation smoke?
Listen with your whole body—Green
Spleenwort fern, growing between cracks
in rocks, speaks what lips can't risk.
It knows it hasn't been forsaken.

To touch the Unalaska Paintbrush, yet
not to crush one flower of its modified leaves.
Here, you can relinquish the wish to be
young again. You want to be old
and wise as Sitka spruces, Western and
Mountain hemlocks of five hundred years,
as prickly as Devil's club so nothing
will ever mess with you again.

Arctic Ice Seals

I don't know it yet
(perhaps it's just as well),
but summer sea ice extent
in the Arctic just north of here
will hit a record low this year.

I could guess this much as I sunbathe
by the lake in this temperate rain forest
while Bearded seals give birth and nurse
pups on dwindling pack ice, and splotchy-
coated Ringed seals do likewise in
snow caves on the verge of collapsing.

As if this isn't enough for them
to contend with, here comes Shell Oil
to drill in ice seal habitat.
Don't tell me this is nature's way,
a few species dying out every day.

Don't say this is about survival
of the fittest. I could almost leap
the world's ties and sit with Han-Shan
among white clouds here in Misty—
forget all about endangered seals.

But if I did, how could I face the Feasts
of Holy Cross and Our Lady of Sorrows,
the Whooping cranes, the dodos?
Dozing here in the sun, among fiords
and tumbling waterfalls, a Whiskered seal
leans close to whisper in my ear, *Listen,*
the sounds entering the lake—snow melt,
fire and grit—a benediction of the heart.

Zinging, stinging wake-up call,
how could I allow the summer sun to lull me
into believing all is well or as it's meant to be?
Weave together what you will—
science, mystery, magic, God—

it all comes down to this: what goes
around comes around; common
courtesy, decency what we need;
to share and share alike; let the moment's
eloquent grief speak for itself: the sea ice
melts; snow caves collapse; then poof!
We're all in this together, sink or swim—
no longer a matter of us or them.

Nudged by an alpine breeze,
I open my eyes to find the snow caps
on rounded ridges surrounding the lake
have shrunk an inch while I dozed
on the shore, the loon pair keeping watch
over their domain and me—a pilgrim
bent on loving the living as fervently
as the dead, praying to be forgiven.

Eulachon

(pronounced "hooligan")

Sure, the salmon
are the star attraction.
But today I turn my attention
to eulachon in the Unuk River
outside Ketchikan. Distant
cousin to salmon, these
nutritious fat-rich fish
nothing to sneeze at.

Esteemed by fishermen, whales
and seals, sea lions and gulls,
porpoises, terns, mink and fox,
river otters and bears, wolves
and wolverines. They, same as
salmon, migrating upstream
to freshwater spawning grounds,
triggered by tide patterns,
light levels, water temperature.

Like salmon, most adults dying
once they reproduce. Providing
a feast for all as they run through
the Tongass along riverbanks—
one of the food chain's vital links.
They and their oil once valued
for bartering along *grease trails*
southeast Alaska to British Columbia.

Prized by Tlingit, Haida, Tsimshian
tribes, this silver fish alive
in my palm all that is made.
Enduring. Reflecting light into my
dark face. I let it leap out of
my hand, continue on its way.

Let others praise the salmon,
all five kinds. I'll lavish affection
on these members of the Smelt family—

pray we never have to count them
among the extinct ones. Their bodies
brilliant as glacial ice, streaking
like lightning—fast and fleeting.
Silence of their passage mingling with
silence of Water ouzel dipping under
the falls—clear water of this bionetwork,
taste of wild wetness infusing my tongue.

How the eulachon lend a sacred air
of continuity to this river, its streams.
An irrepressible urge begins to emerge—
to join them in their revelry of running,
leaping, flying upstream—to be one
with them, wild and born to swim
against the current, against all odds,
let water trickle down my back
as I skim the next fall.

Scaled to perfection, hailed
by men and beasts, eulachon
one way or the other
giving it all they've got.

Glacial Sculpting

Far from all war zones
and refugee camps, dead ends and
hacked-off limbs, you enter
the mist and marvel at the magic,
the mystery of glacial sculpting.
Misty Fiords' rugged terrain, uplift,
glaciation, limited human occupation
till ten thousand years ago.

Cirques at heads of glacial valleys—
amphitheater-like—hollow,
steep-sided, carved into a mountain.
A molten rock solidifies under pressure,
becomes granite. Erosion relieves
that force, expands the rock,
creates cracks in fiord walls,
some standing vertically, others

parallel to slope or cliff face—
some slab or curved sheet exfoliating
(breaking loose) from the outcrop.
Domes, odd shapes (an owl's face) result.
Fractures, overhangs, small ledges—
compliments of the jointing pattern—
for nesting birds whose droppings fertilize
the cliff face, which mosses and lichens grace.

Like an onion being peeled,
a rock mass stripped of concentric
rock slabs from its outer surface.
Granite: composed of micas,
sodium-rich plagioclase,
feldspar, quartz—an intrusive
igneous rock, course-grained.
A joint, a fracture, a crack in bedrock

causing no displacement.
This is about rock metamorphosis—
transformation of texture,
composition, original mineralogy

brought on by pressure, temperature,
loss or gain of chemical compounds.
The granite's natural color concealed
by a solid carpet of rock weed,

mussels and barnacles, tar-black lichen.
Only in the splash zone does it reveal
its silver-grey stunning self.
You'd gladly trade your rubber boots
for the gear of a mermaid. You'd
give up Arctic dreams to stay in Misty
among seals with spectral eyes, and
granite walls with faces like owls.

Where Weighty Glaciers Recede,

isostatic rebound occurs—
terrain rising an inch a year.
Fresh earth emerging along shores.
New life taking root,

natural succession a lesson
not to be missed. Massive Mendenhall
Glacier just the iceberg's tip.
Blue ice split from the glacier's face—

chunks that drift like weighty lace.
But let's go back seven million years:
first small glaciers forming in those
upper elevation watersheds,

transforming V-shaped river valleys
into Us—sharpening, steepening
the ridges' crests, what ice does best.
Earth's climate chilling (more snow falling,

less melting), glaciers extending into lowlands,
coalescing to form deeper ice masses,
etching cliffs into valley walls. Frozen
tide rising, only highest peaks exposed.

Then the climate's milder mode,
ice retreating. Dozens of times,
valley and alpine glaciation. Go back
twenty-five thousand years,

ice extending west of Misty Fiords
cross-continent to Cape Cod.
Go back, fifteen thousand years
the great ice sheet beginning to retreat,

sea levels rising to flood fiords.
Back, ten thousand years, spruce and
hemlocks replacing alder, willow,
tundra vegetation. Six thousand

years, another glacial advance.
Three thousand six hundred years,
Little Ice Age was all the rage
18th to 19th century, scouring and sweeping

away like Judgment Day. Praise
glaciers and fresh earth, blue ice and
ice sheets' retreats, spruce and hemlocks
whose longevity is to be envied.

So much change and adaptability.
Blessed be the rising of terrain,
the infinite falling of snow and rain.
Natural succession made precious

by its fleeting nature. If glaciers
never moved—were as fixed as
rooted trees—would we esteem them
as much as gems?

Full Moon While Flying DFW to Richmond

Red eye, early July,
returning from Alaska—
Juneau, Ketchikan
(Misty Fiords)—where I
practiced echo-location,
ontological insubordination,
considered with every step
along the wet, slippery trail,
each dip of paddle into lake

to my goal to live as an equal
partner with bear and salmon,
raven and eagle, glacier and
old growth forest; to entangle
myself in intricate roots of
Hemlock and Sitka spruce,
in tendrils of Old Man's Beard,
to be insatiable in my hunger
to know loon and humpback whale,

to treat each moss and lichen,
bird and insect with utmost respect.
What did I learn from my brief sojourn?
That I must, at every turn, begin
again in humility and gratitude,
to locate myself in the biosphere,
perceive each species as distant relative.
Alaska taught me what I thought
I already knew—how dependent

and connected we all are. What joy
to recognize the Stellar's jay,
orcas at play—to get so caught up
in their worlds that my own was no
longer separate. Temperate
rainforest singing its refrain,
bears waiting in the lull of late July
for Salmon and Blueberry flowers to fade
and give way to the berries they crave.

A green so lush the only proper response
is a hush of silence, mist over the fiords
like ecstatic chords of mystical music
only audible to ears of the humble.
Alaska put me in my place,
its grace reminding me my species
was an afterthought. Caught
in its eye, having no permanent home,
I was taken in—more than pilgrim,

I sought to enlarge my sapience,
to participate in all of her nature
so reconciliation could occur.
And it did—between me and her
as I leaned out over lakes and Pacific,
observed and listened while glaciers
glistened all around me, their surging
rhythms ancient, echoing,
          all-knowing.

Camino de Santiago

Some places it doesn't take much
faith to believe Rosetti was right—
places where traveling light
is preferred, and listening
with open ears and heart

to storks and hoopoes,
the Milky Way (yes, listen)
is all that's required.
Each morning awakening
on a new patch of holy ground,

far from the spiritless legalism
permeating all religions.
Floating free above fields
of red poppies, forgetting
all hairsplitting theological disputations—

joining in the joyful celebrations
of butterflies fluttering among flowers,
and snails parading down dew-
moistened trails. The Word
lights on one's shoulder,

no longer a heavy boulder.
Treading softly, separating from
all worldly things till the earth's
holy ground transforms one's whole
being into the lover. From then on,

no need of any other way
of walking. Like the bee-eater
escaping the cold north,
now hunting sustenance
in the warm sun.

Blackbirds Falling from the Sky

Blackbirds are falling from the sky,
foaming at their mouths,
and you ask me why
disturbed nature has
unnerved me?

Process physics,
mathematics' chaos theory
reflecting the world—
ecological and weather patterns
governed by nonlinear chaos.

Flapping wings of the butterfly
in Mexico causing air currents to
amplify over San Francisco.
Forget the Brazilian rainforest,
the greenhouse effect. Forget

global apocalypse—concepts too
quotidian now. Blackbirds falling
at your feet. Time to break free
of compassion fatigue, tackle
the politics of environment,

reread Virgil's *Eclogues* and
Shelley's *Epipsychidion,* lament
the loss of landscapes, species,
innocence and wonder.
Time for anger,

contemplation,
disquiet as you sense
your separateness,
sin of trespassing though you
tread as softly as you can.

A mix of exaltation and grief
hits you head on as you observe
nature, every creature—save
yourself—connected.
Arrogance, ignorance, greed—

look how they all lead straight
into polluted waters, despoiled
forests, eroded poisoned soil,
disappeared species. Not even
hanging upside down on a wall

performing prayers and self-
flagellations forty days can save us.
Excluding ourselves from Earth's time-
space continuum, we've become
slow, impervious, dull.

Grant us, Creator of all,
a vision of the universe's
sacredness. Sunflowers,
turn your faces from sun
to blackbirds falling from sky.

Scatter your seeds
among bodies, diseased,
as they fall and die
on desecrated,
holy ground.

Tetrameles Nudiflora

(Spung Tree of Angkor)

There is a tree that says it all—
sprouting out of cracks and chinks
of crumbling temple walls.
It ensnared me right there and then,
miles and miles from Phnom Penh
with its latest Wi-Fi tuk-tuks.
I stood in awe—began to weep—
how one bird can poop out one seed

on an eleventh-century temple roof,
and a majestic tree can sprout, wrapping
its roots about stones, oblivious to frowns
of monkey gods and snakes. How descendants
of that one bird come to nest and rest
among its branches. How the flesh-and-blood
monkeys have a field day as they whoop and play.

How infinity's given a voice as it rises above
stones laid down by man. Elegant and fluid
its roots, indeed a tree to be treasured
though it mercilessly fractures the temple's face.
Haunting and stimulating. Consoling.
What dazzling disintegration its roots have caused.
An opportunist prying into ancient stones' fissures
and cracks in its reach toward heaven.

Like tendrils of a trailing vine, gentle and yet
fierce in its staunch confrontation of man's creation.
A ravishing hold with flare in this country of glorious
lotus blossoms and water lilies, too many amputees
and blood-stained rice paddies. Mesmerized,
I float like a sparkling dust mote among the roots
of the spung and offer my body to be entwined.
Encroaching jungle scene jealousy-green.

Tenacious trees sprung up between centuries of kings
and the Pol Pot regime, between the martyred
and the exiled. This is an ode to the most ostentatious

tree I may ever know. Look how rain clouds mimic
precisely the color of its trailing dangling roots,
how those roots girdle the grey-green stones
of sagging walls. Was there ever a mightier Midas—
turning stagnant stones into flowing veins of white gold?

Just Past Sunset, the Red Fox

caught a brown mouse behind
my dune shack. Our eyes met.
On my part, love at first sight.
From his alert ears to his white-
tipped tail, he was all I had imagined
he would be—handsome, slender,
silent, and shy. In a nanosecond,
I fell under his spell. He lingered,

held my gaze, then circled round the shack
before sauntering past the privy,
hesitating, looking back. Then I lost track
of him as he followed the trail down in
between dunes. I'd been just fine, isolated
for six days. But suddenly, lonely,
I whispered *Please come back.*
But he was gone. Dusk wore on

to night. I counted waves
instead of sheep—the great ones
of the outer ocean approaching
by threes the beach in front of me.
I fell asleep envisioning Red fox padding
across sands, climbing over dunes
to the knee-high forest of pitch pines
and scrub oaks, searching for food.

At dawn I walked out among
new green spears and last year's
dry brown stalks of Beach grass.
My eyes searched hollows,
hoping for a glimpse of him.
A large brown female harrier swooped
low, but Red fox did not show.
Through spring mist and warmth,

I walked back to my shell of a shelter,
the sun barely discernible overhead.
Savoring breakfast, I pondered the dunes—

Sea rockets and Beach peas,
Seaside goldenrod, Salt-spray roses
and bayberries scenting the salt air,
Song sparrow singing for his mate
from the top of a Beach plum.

Walk Gingerly Through Thickets

of salt meadow grass,
fearful of stepping on eggs
of Sharp-tailed sparrows
whose eyes—piercing as arrows—

are keeping watch. See them,
secretive though they be, jumping
out of (then dropping back into)
the grass. Don't bother to ask

why they don't weave nests
of marsh hay, then line them with breast
feathers of gulls the way Bank swallows do
on the Cape's clay outcrops.

Just let them be. Walk gingerly,
pulse of ocean's waves at your back.
Don't crush the S-shaped track
of the snake passing this way before you.

Was it the boldly-striped Ribbon?
or the Garter? Black racer or Hognose
in search of Spadefoot toads?
Walk gingerly through moist air,

suspended between marsh and sky;
take it all in stride—this mineral world
of which you're such an insignificant part.
Watch brown-shelled Marsh snails

climb up blades of grass that sway as
rising waters lap against them, and marvel
at how well equipped each creature is
to live on this outer cape—these snails

with lungs instead of gills, climbing out
of water to breathe. Consider your own
design. Don't waste any more time
residing where you cannot thrive.

Four Nesting Boxes

surround the dune shack,
each one claimed by a pair
of Tree swallows busy

preening and mating,
setting up housekeeping,
sweeping insects from the air.

Song sparrows lustily sing from
tops of Salt-spray rose bushes.
Spring, and love is everywhere.

Breeding season underway,
best reason to be here late May.
Catbirds in plum thickets,

Redwings in bayberries,
Sand martins (Bank swallows)
in the Cape's clay outcrops.

But all is not wine and roses—
interspersed between affection
much aggression. And when Red

fox comes at dusk, poking
his nose into bushes of Beach rose,
I hold my breath.

Dune Forest

When you need a change of scenery,
a little greenery
after days of gazing out
over the ocean,
propped
atop
a foredune in your shack,

keeping track
of whale migrations
and sea birds' peregrinations;
when you've memorized
the tides
and the calls of each shorebird—
from the tern's stern screams

to the plover's plaintive pipes,
the Greater yellowleg's *tew-tew-tew,*
the gull's laughs—
walk into the troughs
between dunes,
into the forest of twisted Pitch pines
and pygmy Scrub oaks

where drops of salt spray pooling on tips
of trees kill tender new growth.
Yet sprouting still
in barren sand enriched
by fallen needles,
grass and flower seeds dispersed
by birds and wind.

Rabbits drawn to nibble on Poverty grass,
then foxes to hunt the rabbits and
Red squirrels. Anthills
and lichens abound.
Blueberry bushes like vines,
Poison ivy that winds
around trunks, and cherries

among the pines.
Scent of resin.
Whisper of leaves as they breathe
in the faintest sea breeze
blowing across the dunes,
reminding you
the ocean is still in view.

Migrations

Contemplating wings,
I think of miraculous
mysterious migrations,
of species and ecosystems
in jeopardy: butterflies;

hummingbirds; Snow geese;
bats—four million from Mexico
to Texas and back each year—
controlling insects, dispersing seeds.
Tens of millions of monarchs

flying central Mexico to as far north
as Canada—five generational waves,
the last returning to a place they've
never been two thousand miles away.
The five-foot Whooping crane

voyaging twenty-four hundred miles
from Canada's boreal forest to winter
along the Texas coast—prairies,
wetlands, floodplains what they need most
as they refuel and rest along the way.

Mulling over migration highways
endangered by new roads and houses,
shopping malls and suburban sprawl,
I awaken to the mystery, imagine
making such a journey year after year,

caught up in the sacred balance. Hear
the haunted honking of geese passing over
in their faultless V. See
thousands of monarchs alight on limbs
to rest until the next leg of their flight.

Envisioning wings, I find the door.
Spring, autumn passages.
Messages of hope, each lifting off,
each return. Who would not yearn
for wings and the migratory instinct?

If only one Rufous hummer
arrives in Misty Fiords this summer
to feast on Salmon and Blueberries,
it'll be reason enough to not give up.

Meditation on Holiness

On this Good Friday,
Purim, first day of the Vernal
Equinox, Worm Moon Day all
wrapped into one, Mother
Teresa's words weigh on the mind:
Holiness no luxury for the few
...obligation for all.
This point of equal balance,
light and dark, oleander scenting
the garden, Father of flowers having

scattered them and nasturtium all
around—my little patch of earth
transformed into holy ground,
I want to oblige: be like Esther
pleading for her people, petition China
to free Tibet; be like oleander spreading
the sweet scent of hope in life after death,
enlivening this Arabian Desert with color,
offering sustenance to the hungry;
this Worm Moon Day, to pray

for the soil as farmers toil to cut furrows,
run ploughshares, sow seed; this
Good Friday, to rest on the soil's rich
realm, marvel yet again how death has
nurtured new life. Surely no saint—
too full of doubt, afraid still every year
to let the world die so it can rise
yet again—still, in my desert,
I sing the Earth, give thanks for yet

another rebirth, follow the dragonflies
with their gleaming, large-pupiled eyes—
leave behind all my vainglorious pursuits
to take on their humble task: poised
flame-bright, unwavering, on the tip
of a yellow-green pond weed offering
thanks for sun, pond, bull thistle—

holiness accrued to me only as I
acknowledge I am creation's clay,
made of feldspar, scoured by dust-laden,
spirit-driven winds.

How to Be Courageously Simple

> *Without courage, we can never attain*
> *to true simplicity.* —Thomas Merton

Whatever you do,
don't do what they expect you to.
Consider the most rational,
practical, lucrative choice,
then shelve it—no, better,

throw it over the cliff.
When they warn,
Keep a stiff upper lip,
make a deliberate effort
to make yours quiver.

Whatever they expect you
to deliver, come through
with the opposite. When
they say run, sit. When they
advise, *Buy this and that,*

sell all you have and give to the poor.
You've heard this all before,
and though something about it
entices you, you cannot bring yourself
to do what would lead to a life

free of all their trappings.
What with all your mappings
of simplicity's routes, you've
given in to the deadly doubts.
But there's still time:

get out, get out!
Be courageous—
do the simply outrageous
that will shock them
and liberate you.

Suggested Companions

To walk the middle path,
keep company with one who's dying

and one who's just come into
this world, with one whose pastime

is hunting and one who's converted
to Tibetan Buddhism—won't kill

even a flea. Keep company with caribou
on their frozen tundra and butterflies

flittering on invisible air currents,
with raven acrobats performing for free

and Liguus snails trekking up
smooth-barked trails of hammock

trees, with a solitary shepherd of
flock and flute and a murder of

supreme court judges decked out
in their crow-black robes, with

goldenrod rustling—rising and
bowing before the breeze—

and the stark, silent, still mountain
accepting the weathering of bacteria

and plants bent on reducing it
to rubble.

Created Together

The universe came into being with us together;
with us, all things are one. —Chuang Tzu

Because we were created together,
because its existence depends on me
and mine on it, because when it bleeds
I bleed, what it needs I need,

because its creatures—all except for Homo
sapiens—are without sin, doing nothing
to defile Earth—shells and pearls on a
thousand shores, inside a thousand oysters
more lustrous than man's meager achievements
and attempts to incite ecstasy—even Abu
Sa'id's poetry,

because it's a master of silence,
is incapable of hate, cradles its anemones
in the bosom of its seas more precious
than any Zen heaven,

because it keeps its opinions
to itself—doesn't try to push its serenity
on me, yet neither does it withhold its
treasures,

because it forgives how we intrude,
nudges us to make amends by paying
attention to the minutest mysteries,
shows how to remain as still and silent
as its egrets and herons on a thousand
shores,

I bow down to all created things, to
this universe where all is one.

Into Vastness and Freedom

In Memory of American Catholic nun
Sister Dorothy Stang, murdered February 2005
in the Brazilian Amazon

Today if I could, I surely would
go seaward into vastness and freedom.
Our dreams of safety must disappear.
I hear Auden's words ring crystal-clear
as I mourn the murder of an aging nun

in the Brazilian Amazon who took on
the poor man's struggle for land
and livelihood—lived out her faith.
Soon to venture into a realm that's unsafe,
I hear loved ones plead, *Don't be hasty in*

risking your life—so much misery and strife
everywhere. You could just as well stay here
as go there to save the world. Why take it upon
your aging shoulders—why carry other people's
boulders up the mountain?

Let each one fight her own battle;
you should stay right here in Seattle.
Ah, but tomorrow they may come for us.
I can't resist—must attempt to be His
presence, save the earth one species, world

one person at a time, even if she calls to me
from Sudan or Afghanistan. Why not this very
day go seaward into vastness and freedom?
Nothing to stop me now that 9/11's burst
the bubble dream of safety.

Letting Go

Don't be blinded
by your clinging.
Look how it always leads
to neurotic behavior,
ego-fixation. Emulate
nature letting go
season after season.
Be like snow: even though
it gives the illusion of clinging
to bare limbs and ledges,
rooftops and bridges,
it's all the while waiting
for the sun to come and melt it
molecule by molecule,
freeing it from the illusion
of clinging.

Emulate the child swinging—
notice how with every thrust
of body and soul into the air,
she indubitably is reaching for
anywhere beyond the wooden seat
and the ropes of hemp her hands
are gripping. She is not clinging,
joyfully resisting gravity's hold,
every swinging moment
a proclamation of liberation
from clinging to the earth.

Emulate the tides—
their rhythm and rhyme
as they rise and subside,
clinging neither to shore
nor to ocean's deep dark floor,
relinquishing every hidden
treasure, every last ornament.

Lastly, emulate the meadowlark:
when she sings, she clings neither
to branch nor blossom—her sweetest
song sung on the wing between
earth and heaven.

Prophet or Flamingo

If given a choice
(and when not, take it!),
choose desert over temple,
margins over centers.
Aspire to being prophet
or flamingo, follow Gandhi's
and Francis's footsteps—
listen with open heart
to the animals, preach to the birds.

Spend daylight hours waltzing
and flitting about butterfly-like
among flowers, evenings
trailing behind a lunar moth.
Take nothing for granted.
Praise dewdrops as prolifically
as snowflakes. Face facts:
humans the only ones to flout
heaven, breaking the harmony.

Fight like an avenging warrior
to save the Everglades. Never fancy
yourself more precious than the unfallen,
undepraved alligator. Boldly break
with tradition: if impositioned by loss,
don't don black. Escape from silk,
crepe, suffocating veils. Don't hang
a black-ribboned wreath on the door.
What on earth for?

Instead, choose scarlet or orange—blaze
like black gum leaves in their final days.
Rise before dawn to graze with deer,
drink from their pond, hear bird's
first song as assurance here and now—
this very day—is eternity no matter what
the skeptics say. Leap like gazelle
across golden meadow into blessed
resined woods of decay and shadow.

Invisible

is what I'd be
if it were left up to me.
Odorless
or, like the pitch pine,
aromatic and elastic
in the path of sea wind.
Graceful as dragonfly,
melodious as a Persian
nightingale.
Pliant as bamboo.

I'd shoot up improbably
through hard-packed sand
like that deep bright blue
Blepharis ciliaris.
I'd be the sudden flash
of a white-breasted king-
fisher in an olive grove.
I'd be light and fleet
as a gazelle, ready at any
moment to leap away
at the least disturbance
of peace. Serene and silent
I'd be, like the desert fox
surveying his kingdom
sunrise, sunset from the top
of a violet-tipped barchan
dune. I'd be content
and matter-of-fact as the cat
dozing in her favorite sunspot
as if she has nothing more
important to do all day.

Migratory I'd be,
part of the V-formation—
that one who always strays
just a tad for comic relief
and causes at least one
person on the traffic-jammed
street below to lift her eyes
to the skies and smile.

Lessons in Grasses and Trees

Love is never so intense as when it is silent.
—Fr. Benson, Founder, Society of St. John the Evangelist

Who better to teach silence and stillness
than Earth: resignation in autumn, rebirth
in spring? In the heart of the Kansas Flint Hills,
a prairie of tall grasses 250 million years old—
inland seas laying down limestone beds,

flint and shale, erosion sculpting steep-sided
terraced table lands—I make a request:
in my final silence, ashes windswept over
rivers, hills, prairies, let my reincarnation be
as fish, long-legged wading birds, grasses, trees.

Let my ashes, like the insects' carcasses,
fertilize. But while still alive, let me fully
realize the whole scope of the silent tree:
air, water, sunlight, roots and earth, insects,
fungi, bird with its song and droppings,

leaf, blossom, bole, balm of bark, wind that
bends and shapes—sometimes breaks—the limb.
Silent love—tree, sawgrass prairie, grassy river—
seepages of water rising rainy season, swaying
reeds to which snails cling, sedges

with their sword-sharp edges red-winged
blackbirds know just how to tip-toe around.
Intensity of silent love—verification
of eternity there for all to see in the still
silent solitude of the great blue heron.

Hawk-like, I perch on lips
of cliffs and slender ledges, river
banks and tips of sedges dragonfly-
like—loving as silently and intensely
as I'm loved.

Holy Ground

Holy—every part of it.

What rises up from it:
poised serene trees,
grasses and sedges—
some with blade-sharp edges—
responding to sun,
rain and breeze.

What lies on it unmovable,
and yet you can detect a heartbeat:
stones and mountains.

Over it: shimmering fireflies
and ravens, clouds and mists,
cremation smoke.

Under it: root systems, seeds
of plants and trees, mangos, avocados,
burrows of a million creatures.

Through it: rivers and streams.

What teems across it:
microscopic lives, and the larger
ones—a feast for our eyes.

What nourishes it: sun and rain,
scattered leaves, fallen blossoms
decaying carcasses of mammals,
birds, insects.

Treading softly so as not to miss
the holiness of confederated
dependencies: air, water, soil—
holiness of the natural order.

Treading softly, no rush,
no noisy chatter. Letting the hush
of Earth's form and matter
wash over me till I'm born again,
cleansed of every sin against her.

Notes

"Jazirat Umm Tais Preserve": "I turned around, and the water was closing all around like a glove..." from "Crystal" by Fleetwood Mac; Kimiko Hahn, "The Calf," *Earshot* (Hanging Loose Press, 1992); "Getting and spending, we lay waste our powers..." from "The World Is Too Much with Us" by William Wordsworth

"Mangrove Forest, Umm Tais National Park": *halos,* derived from the Greek word for salt

"Everglades: Day One": Job's suggestion, from Job 12:7-8; "though we cut it with our swords" from "A Farewell to Secretary Shuyun at the Xietiao Villa in Xuanzhou" by Li Po

"Pa-hay-okee": the Everglades, called by the Seminole Indians *Pa-hay-okee,* meaning grassy waters

"Nooya Lake": "in complicity with things as they happen" from Lyn Hejinian's *Happily* (The Post-Apollo Press, 2000)

"Conducting Research in Misty": "'Beauty is truth, truth beauty'—that is all..." from "Ode on a Grecian Urn" by John Keats; "Truth is one," a Buddhist adage

Acknowledgments

I am grateful to the editors of the following journals, in which some of these poems first appeared, at times in slightly different versions.

American Chordata: "Glacial Sculpting"
Assisi, Spring 2011: "How to Be Courageously Simple"
Comstock Review: "Invisible"
Connotation Press: An Online Artifact: "Pa-hay-okee"
Crab Orchard Review: "In the Company of Alligators"
Flyway: Journal of Writing and Environment: "Beggar in the
    Everglades"
ISLE: Interdisciplinary Studies in Literature and Environment:
    "Celestial Cathedral," "Desert Monitor Lizard," "Pa-hay-okee"
MacGuffin: "Winstanley Lake, Misty Fiords (Revillagigedo Island)"
Peace & Freedom: "Obligation"
Plainsongs: "Every August"
Poetry Salzburg Review: "Tetrameles Nudiflora"
Portland Review: "Everglades: Day One"
Quiddity: "Existence Is Light"
Southern Women's Review: "If You Doubt"
Spillway/Tebot Bach: "Kin to All of Nature"
The Cresset: "Meditation on Holiness"
The Wayfarer: A Journal of Contemplative Literature: "Dune Forest,"
    "Four Nesting Boxes"
Written River: A Journal of Eco-Poetics: "Full Moon While Flying DFW
    to Richmond," "Learning to Tread Softly," "Nooya Lake, Misty Fiords"

"Beggar in the Everglades," "Holy Ground," and "Pa-hay-okee" appeared in *ECOTHEE: Ecological Theology and Environmental Ethics* (Orthodox Academy of Crete Publications, 2009).

"Migrations" appeared in *Poised in Flight Anthology* (Kind of a Hurricane Press, 2013).

"Where Weighty Glaciers Recede" appeared in *Elementary My Dear Anthology* (Kind of a Hurricane Press, 2015).

"Just Past Sunset, the Red Fox" received a National Honorable Mention, Joe Gouveia Outermost Poetry Contest, WOMR/WFMR Community Radio of Cape Cod, 2016. "Letting Go" received 3rd prize, Artists Embassy International/Dancing Poetry Contest 2010. "Lunchtime Along the

Tideline" received 2nd prize in Artists Embassy International's 2009 Dancing Poetry Contest. "Invisible" received 3rd prize in Artists Embassy International's Dancing Poetry Contest 2009. "Obligation" ranked among the top 5 entries in Peace & Freedom Press's *Animals & Wildlife Poetry* competition, 2009. "In the Company of Alligators," "Beggar in the Everglades," and "Everglades: Day One" were chosen for the National Park Service's *Through Your Eyes* web multimedia exhibitions (2013). "Full Moon While Flying DFW to Richmond," "Winstanley Lake, Misty Fiords (Revillagigedo Island," and "Nooya Lake, Misty Fiords" were chosen for the *Voices of the Wilderness* traveling art exhibit 2014, Alaska U.S. Forest Service. "Just Past Sunset, the Red Fox" and "Walk Gingerly Through Thickets" were chosen for the 2013 Truro Center for the Arts at Castle Hill OCARC Show (Outer Cape Artist Residence Coalition), Truro, MA.

The following poem appeared in the chapbook *Desert Ecology—Lessons and Visions* (Finishing Line Press, 2014): "Every August."

The following poems appeared in the chapbook *Beggar in the Everglades* (Finishing Line Press, 2015): "Everglades: Day One," "In the Company of Alligators," "Beggar in the Everglades," "Existence Is Light," "Celestial Cathedral," "If You Doubt," "Kin to All of Nature," and "Pa-hay-okee."

About FutureCycle Press

FutureCycle Press is dedicated to publishing lasting English-language poetry books, chapbooks, and anthologies in both print-on-demand and Kindle ebook formats. Founded in 2007 by long-time independent editor/publishers and partners Diane Kistner and Robert S. King, the press incorporated as a nonprofit in 2012. A number of our editors are distinguished poets and writers in their own right, and we have been actively involved in the small press movement going back to the early seventies.

The FutureCycle Poetry Book Prize and honorarium is awarded annually for the best full-length volume of poetry we publish in a calendar year. Introduced in 2013, our Good Works projects are anthologies devoted to issues of universal significance, with all proceeds donated to a related worthy cause. Our Selected Poems series highlights contemporary poets with a substantial body of work to their credit; with this series we strive to resurrect work that has had limited distribution and is now out of print.

We are dedicated to giving all of the authors we publish the care their work deserves, making our catalog of titles the most diverse and distinguished it can be, and paying forward any earnings to fund more great books.

We've learned a few things about independent publishing over the years. We've also evolved a unique, resilient publishing model that allows us to focus mainly on vetting and preserving for posterity poetry collections of exceptional quality without becoming overwhelmed with bookkeeping and mailing, fundraising activities, or taxing editorial and production "bubbles." To find out more about what we are doing, come see us at www.futurecycle.org.

The FutureCycle Poetry Book Prize

All full-length volumes of poetry published by FutureCycle Press in a given calendar year are considered for the annual FutureCycle Poetry Book Prize. This allows us to consider each submission on its own merits, outside of the context of a contest. Too, the judges see the finished book, which will have benefitted from the beautiful book design and strong editorial gloss we are famous for.

The book ranked the best in judging is announced as the prize-winner in the subsequent year. There is no fixed monetary award; instead, the winning poet receives an honorarium of 20% of the total net royalties from all poetry books and chapbooks the press sold online in the year the winning book was published. The winner is also accorded the honor of being on the panel of judges for the next year's competition; all judges receive copies of all contending books to keep for their personal library.

9 781942 371489